Choose a topic and start to practise writing. Each booklet has a theme to help you start to write…stories, reports, articles, letters and many more. Start collecting them now.

Guinea Pig creative writing booklets also provide extra practice for children who have completed:

- Creative Story Writing ISBN: 9780955831508
- Persuasive Writing & Argument ISBN: 9780955831515
- Information Writing ISBN: 9780955831522

They are for:

* children who are working at Key Stage 2 of the National Curriculum, levels 3-5 (in Years 5 and 6 of primary school),
* children who are working at Key Stage 3, levels 3-5 (Years 7 and 8 of Secondary School).

They provide practice for all 9-13 year olds, especially children taking 11+ examinations.

© **Copyright 2011**

This pack may not under any circumstances be photocopied, without the prior consent of the publisher.

Written by Sally A Jones and Amanda C Jones

Published by GUINEA PIG EDUCATION

2 Cobs Way,
New Haw,
Addlestone,
Surrey,
KT15 3AF.

www.guineapigeducation.co.uk

First things first...
Let's **learn** how to *write* to persuade.

When you *write* to **persuade**:

- you convince people to do something or believe in something

- you can exaggerate to get other people to agree with your view.

You must decide:

1. Who will be my target audience?

2. Who will read this writing?

3. What is the purpose of my writing?

Let's persuade people to go out for the day and take their children.

You must speak to the reader directly - *'if you're dotty about dolphins...'*

You must use cool words - admirable adjectives and nouns -
'dazzling day out,' 'scrumptious bird shaped biscuits,' the softest feathers'

You must use vibrant verbs and adverbs -
'The ostriches were striding along/strutting proudly.'

You must involve your reader so they agree with your opinions -
'We will teach you much about these delightful creatures.'

Use a non-fiction writing plan:

PARAGRAPH 1 • Write a memorable opening sentence appealing to your reader. • Introduce some facts about your chosen subject.	• Use techniques like alliteration - (d) sounds *'dazzling day out.'* • Use imperatives - *'come'*, *'bring'*
PARAGRAPH 2, 3, 4... • Write down some points you want to make in an order. • Write in detail developing your points.	**Remember:** • Use connectives or conjunctions: - and or but *(to join compound sentences)* - or, so, if, when, while, after, before, because, unless, until, whereas, although *(to join complex sentences)* - use pronouns - who, which, whose, what, that - to link ideas use - firstly, later, therefore, on the other hand, at that moment, by this time, next, soon... • Use a range of sentences – simple, compound and complex sentences
Conclusion • Draw all your ideas together in a conclusion.	• Use a memorable slogan.

'DARING Dolphin Day Out'

A dazzling day out for all you dolphin fans, especially those who dare to dive or swim with these delightful creatures.

Now the owners need a lavish information leaflet, to persuade people to come and experience this wild and watery place. They have given you this job: first, you must design a plan of the centre. Then, you must produce some persuasive writing to tell people what they will see and do there.

You should include:

- reasons why people should visit the centre…

- what there is to see and do there?

- any other useful information…

Make a plan of the 'Daring Dolphin Day Out Centre'. Include an entrance and exit, the different attractions, the café and the shop. What else would be there?

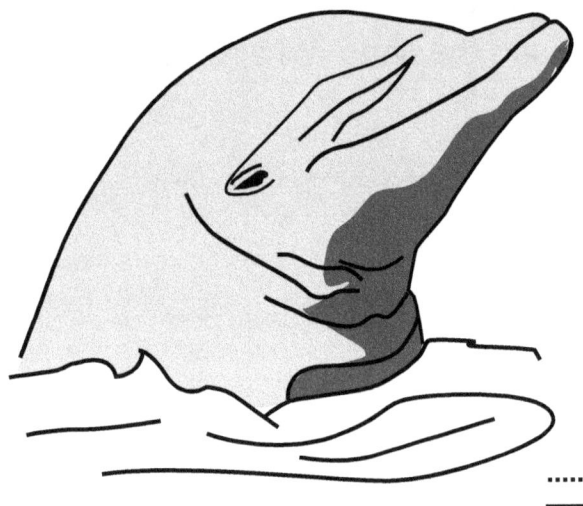

If you're dotty about dolphins, come and experience a <u>dazzling</u> day out at our new <u>*DOLPHIN*</u> CENTRE.

You will learn so much about these delightful creatures. Bring the whole family to the centre, so they can enjoy a day out they'll never forget. Teachers, if you bring your class, they will learn so much. The children will be able to fill in our fun work sheets as they observe the behaviour of these delightful animals up close.

When you come to our centre, you must experience swimming with the dolphins. It would be simply amazing to tell your friends you've been diving deep in the blue water with these gentle creatures. Even if you dare not come in such close contact with our friendly dolphins like Borris or Bethan, you can still watch them perform amazing tricks in the pool, with their trainer, during our daily dolphin show.

Our education centre has a wealth of literature on dolphin behaviour. You can watch some D.V.D clips on how dolphins live in their natural environment or enjoy a showcase of information on endangered wildlife threatened by extinction.

Beside this, there are walks through lovely gardens on your way to the aquarium, which houses hundreds of exotic colourful fish.

When you feel like a break, the Dolphin Café serves freshly made hot drinks in dolphin shaped mugs. It has an amazing selection of pasties and hot meals, with some sensational animal character cakes and biscuits. Definitely worth a try!

Don't forget to call in at our dolphin shop. Take home one of our special ornaments to decorate your home and remind you of your visit.

Where are we?
We are easy to find. Come off the M26 motorway at junction 20 and then follow the signs.

<u>Cost</u>

Adults - £10.00

Children (under 16) £7.50

<u>Opening Times</u>

Summer time – 9am – 6pm

Wintertime – 9am – 4pm

Interesting dolphin facts:

- Dolphins belong to a group of whales called 'toothed whales'. The killer whale comes from this family.

- They are aquatic, warm-blooded mammals that live in the sea or ocean. Dolphins are found all over the world – from the icy seas of the Arctic and Antarctic to the tropical oceans. Some species are even found in the Amazon River.

- A dolphin has a streamlined body, smooth skin, no hair and no ears. Under the dolphin's smooth skin, there is a layer of fat or blubber which helps to keep him warm.

- To swim, they push down with their powerful tail fin and steer with their flippers.

- The colour of their bodies helps camouflage them in the water, so they can't be seen by predators.

- Dolphins can stay under water for a long time. Some dolphins can live underwater for as long as 30 minutes. They have a blowhole on top of their head, so they can come to the surface and breathe.

- Dolphins are social creatures and live in family groups called schools. Often a family will consist of a grandmother, a daughter and her children. They hunt for food together.

- To locate prey, they send out a series of clicks from their throats (echolocation), which bounce off shoals of fish ahead and returns to the dolphin's ear. Fish and squid are their favourite foods.

- They are fast, agile swimmers. They leap out of the water and perform somersaults. Together, they glide across the water to communicate with other dolphins. This is why they enjoy swimming with humans.

- Sometimes a dolphin pushes his head out of the water, looking for food or land.

- Dolphins are very intelligent creatures. In fact, they have an IQ as high as a human toddler!

> ● Have a go at writing a persuasive leaflet, persuading people to visit 'The Dolphin Day Out Centre'.
>
> • Use the information on this page to help you write an informative leaflet about dolphins.

Write your persuasive leaflet here.

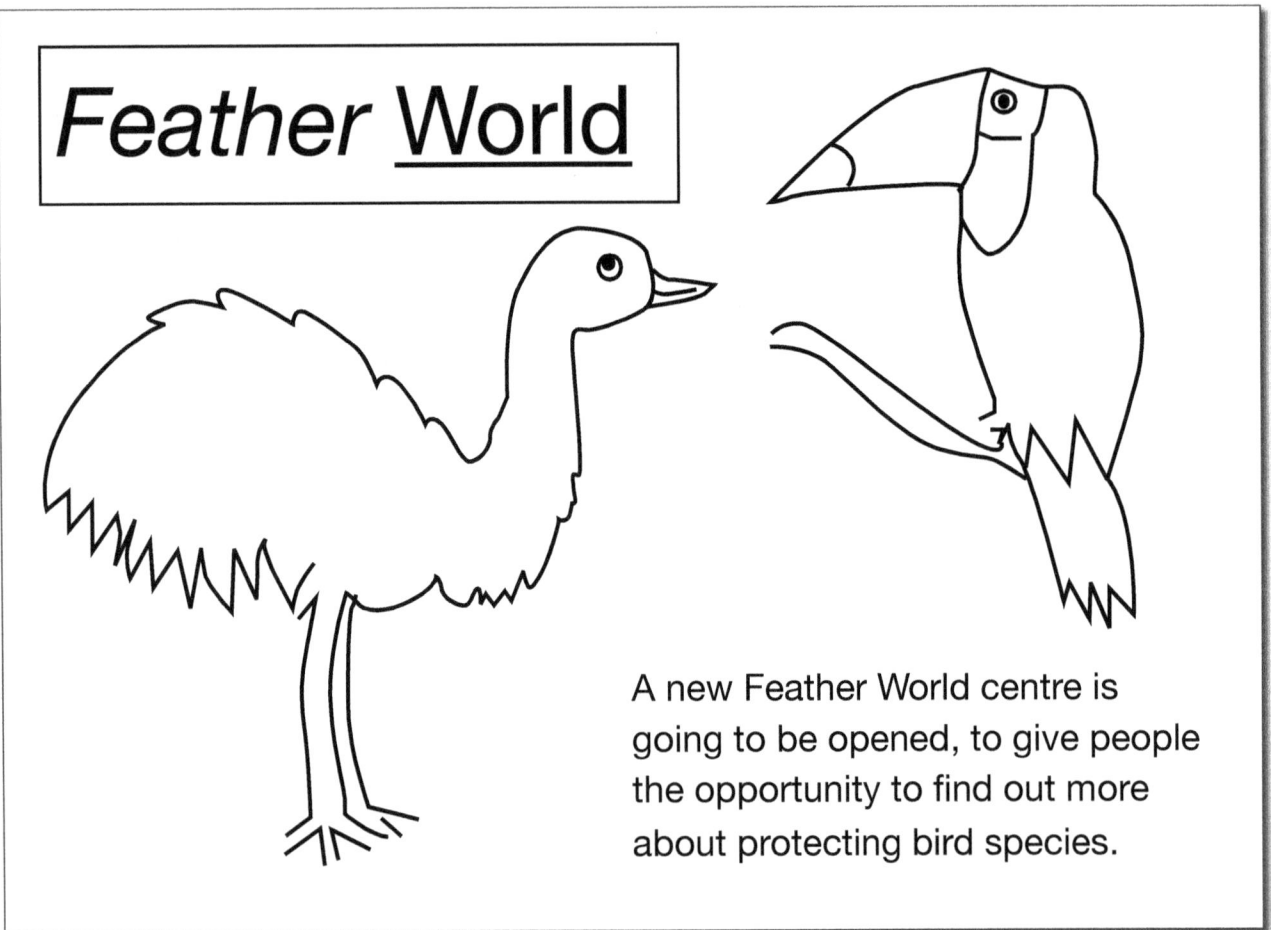

Feather World

A new Feather World centre is going to be opened, to give people the opportunity to find out more about protecting bird species.

The owners have asked you to write a persuasive leaflet to persuade people to come to the centre. A plan of the bird centre has been drawn up to put in the leaflet. Your task is to do the writing, which will tell people what there is to see and do there.

Think about the purpose of the leaflet:

- Who will the reader be?

- Give some reasons why people should come…

- Say what they will see and do when they are there…

- Give other information….

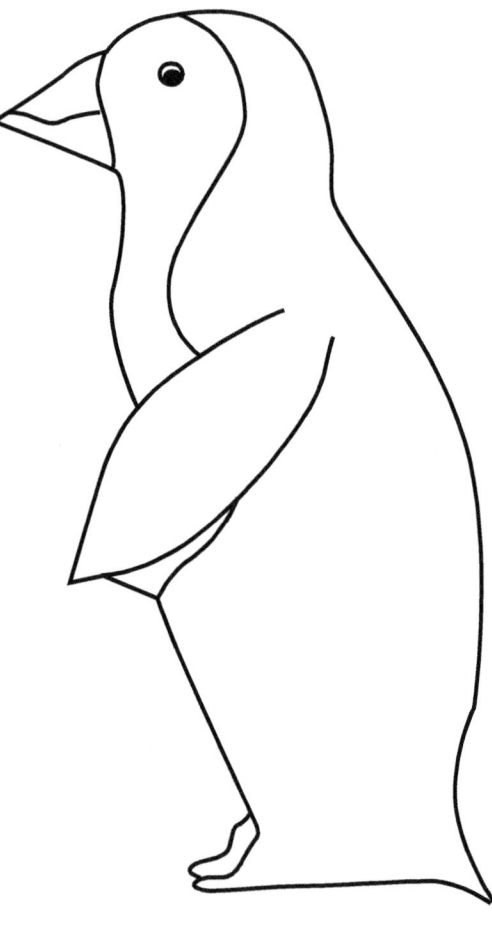

Here are some ideas for writing persuasive sentences:

Come and visit...

Teachers will find it a valuable educational experience.

Our birds are ever so friendly...

You will adore our owl family.

Spend time talking to our pretty parrots and clever cockatoo. They may even talk back to you!

Experience a super train ride round the amazing countryside and see birds in their natural environment.

See you again soon.

Watch the falcon dive down from a great height to catch a mouse.

Stare at a cockatoo and see him lower his feathery crest. You'll know he's feeling threatened.

Have fun finding out about...

A day out you'll never forget

They will feed from your hand...

Our baby owls have soft, fluffy feathers.

Enjoy being a keeper for a day and help us out at 'feeding time'.

Visit our café. Treat yourself to one or more of our scrumptious bird shaped biscuits.

See birds of prey soar into the air at the flying demonstration.

Talk to an active, sociable and noisy bird – the parrot. He is very colourful. Hear him screech loudly to communicate with other birds. He will repeat your speech, because he enjoys talking to you.

Become aware of deforestation and capturing wild parrots for the pet trade, which has made some parrots become extinct.

You can bring all the family.

Have fun getting to know our terrific toucan.

Their feathers are such brilliant colours...

You will learn some incredible facts.

Make friends with our flamboyant flamingos, see strutting ostriches and meet – giddy goat and porky pig at animal farm.

In our shop, you will be able to buy the perfect gift to remember your visit.

Observe the hooked beak, sharp talons, piercing eyes and huge powerful wings used to hunt down prey.

Hold out some fruit or nuts and he'll clamber down from his perch, grasp the wires with his talons and take food from your hand with his beak.

Coo over the owls with their three babies, but watch them use their sharp claws to grasp a mouse, a vole, or even a shrew and then swallow it down in one gulp.

Can you find an opinion? *(the writers viewpoint which may not be true)*

Facts inform the reader about things that are true.

Now, write your persuasive leaflet. Include an introduction, two or three paragraphs of information and a conclusion. Think about layout and pictures, headings and fonts.

> Read through the ideas of things you can see and do at Feather World. Choose which ones you want to use. Structure them (organise them into a sensible order.)

Visit Mandelieu la Napoule

BEACHES

The wonderful, warm Mediterranean climate makes it a good place for sunbathing on white sands. Swim in the sparkling, blue sea which is ideal for snorkelling.

HOTELS

There is 5* hotel accommodation or self-catering apartments by the River Siagne which is only a short walk to the sea. You may prefer to camp. You can hire a tent at the campsite, which is close to the bustling town centre.

THINGS TO DO

Take a brisk walk along the rocks to see the castle of La Napoule, which was built in 1390 and is perched on the rocks. Walk at high tide and get splashed by the waves, but it is worth seeing the spectacular views.

FOOD

Local restaurants serve delicious local specialities. Enjoy fresh fish, cooked in the Provencial style or boiled muscles. For a treat, why not try some scrumptious lavender flavoured ice cream.

Write a travel brochure about your own holiday destination. Fold a piece of A4 paper into three equal pieces to form a holiday brochure.

Organise your writing under headings or sub headings. Use **bold** print:

- *to make the facts stand out*

- *to catch the readers attention*

- *to help the reader find facts quickly*

- *to present information clearly.*

Remember the leaflets <u>PURPOSE</u> is to <u>PERSUADE</u>.

In a non-fiction text you will find:

- *bullet points*

- *different fonts*

- *headings and subheadings*

- *diagrams and charts*

- *illustrations to explain the text*

- *captions - words that explain a photo*

Did you know…

Words like:

   <u>Take</u> a walk

   <u>Eat</u> fresh fish

   <u>Visit</u> Mandelieu la Napoule

are **imperatives**.
They give instructions.

Anna Maria writes...

Come and enjoy soft, sandy beaches, clear blue skies and a refreshing cocktail by your side. If you want all of this and much more from your holiday, then come to Romania - the ultimate summer holiday destination. You will get cheap flights from 'Tarom' airlines, which will get you there in no time!

Romania is a country, which has kept most of its traditional charm, as well as being an authentic 'beach party hot spot'. Constanta, is one of Romania's sea breezed coastal towns. It has five star hotels, just a stones throw away from the beach and all offer fabulous views of the Black Sea from your bedroom window.

You can visit the city centre, which is only ten minutes away, by the classic tourist double-decker buses. There, you can dine in one of the excellent rated restaurants or the Italian styled cafes, overlooking the beautiful sea on the harbour's Monte Carlo white cliffs. Why not spoil yourself, by reserving a day to go to the city wall?

If you are a quiet type of person, who likes no noise and disturbances, then rent a first class quality apartment by Lake Ovidiu (opposite the Black Sea), which is magnificent for peaceful fishing and calm sailing.

What are you waiting for? Your cocktails calling you!

Now write a persuasive article for a magazine about your own holiday destination.

Now write to persuade people to visit an island called Bayukade – off Istanbul in Turkey. Use the following notes to help you:

- *you travel there by boat*
- *it is one of several idyllic islands*
- *it is a 30 minutes sail from Istanbul*
- *it is hot - 40 degrees in summer*

It has:

- *sandy beaches and blue sky*
- *quaint, busy streets*
- *tourist shops in the bazaar, selling souvenirs – like magnets and bracelets and pottery*

What else can you do?

- *play with cute 'street kittens' and look at lazy 'street dogs'*
- *sit and eat local fish in a restaurant by the harbour*
- *choose from a plate of food from the delicious seafood tray*
- *throw left over fish bones and skin to the sea gulls*
- *relax and sip strong Turkish tea in dainty cups*
- *munch freshly picked walnuts*
- *go back in time and take a trip by horse and cart round the island - there are no cars on the island*
- *climb to the top of a mountain, which is about a thirty minute walk*
- *photograph breathtaking scenery*
- *see an ancient church, with lots of old paintings and relics*
- *if you're lucky, see dolphins and turtles in the sea*

Write what you have planned here.

Now, imagine you are on holiday. Use your imagination to write a post card. Use the information in the travel writing on the following page and the questions below to help you.

Where are you on holiday?	You will never guess where…
	I am on holiday at…
Who are you with?	It is in…
	I'm on holiday with…
What is the weather like?	The weather is…
Where are you staying?	The hotel is…
	It has…
What is the food like?	The food is…(delicious), (tasty)
	I'm sharing a room with…
What have you seen/done?	Yesterday I explored…
	I visited…
	swam…
How do you feel about it?	climbed…
Are you enjoying yourself?	Today I am going to…
	Tomorrow…
I wish you were here so…	

Dear ....,

You will never guess where I have been for the last two weeks. I am on holiday on the ....
.... staying at ....
It is ....

I've had a wonderful time exploring the ....
....
....
I have been snorkelling in ....
.... which is ....
My family visited ....
....
..................The weather is..............
....

The food is the most delicious food I've ever tasted, especially the ....
.... My favourite restaurant has ....

The best thing about the holiday is
When I ....
....
....

I will tell you more about it when I get home.

         Love,

         ....

....

....

....

....

....

WISH YOU WERE HERE...

Write your postcard here.

www.ingramcontent.com/pod-product-compliance
Lightning Source LLC
LaVergne TN
LVHW082244060526
838200LV00046B/2053